by Iain Gray

Lang**Syne**

PUBLISHING

WRITING *to* REMEMBER

Lang**Syne**

PUBLISHING

WRITING *to* REMEMBER

79 Main Street, Newtongrange,
Midlothian EH22 4NA
Tel: 0131 344 0414
E-mail: info@lang-syne.co.uk
www.langsyneshop.co.uk

Design by Dorothy Meikle
Printed by Printwell Ltd
© Lang Syne Publishers Ltd 2022

ISBN 978-1-85217-205-3

Wilson

MOTTO:
Always watchful.

CREST:
A demi-lion.

RELATED NAMES INCLUDE:
Wiley
Willie
Wilsone
Wilsoun
Wylie
Wyllie
Wylson

Echoes of a far distant past
can still be found in most names

Chapter one:

Origins of Scottish surnames

by George Forbes

It all began with the Normans.

For it was they who introduced surnames into common usage more than a thousand years ago, initially based on the title of their estates, local villages and chateaux in France to distinguish and identify these landholdings, usually acquired at the point of a bloodstained sword.

Such grand descriptions also helped enhance the prestige of these arrogant warlords and generally glorify their lofty positions high above the humble serfs slaving away below in the pecking order who only had single names, often with Biblical connotations as in Pierre and Jacques.

The only descriptive distinctions among this peasantry concerned their occupations, like Pierre the swineherd or Jacques the ferryman.

The Normans themselves were originally Vikings (or Northmen) who raided, colonised and eventually settled down around the French coastline.

They had sailed up the Seine in their longboats in 900AD under their ferocious leader Rollo and ruled the roost in north east France before sailing over to conquer England, bringing their relatively new tradition of having surnames with them.

It took another hundred years for the Normans to percolate northwards and surnames did not begin to appear in Scotland until the thirteenth century.

These adventurous knights brought an aura of chivalry with them and it was said no damsel of any distinction would marry a man unless he had at least two names.

The family names included that of Scotland's great hero Robert De Brus and his compatriots were warriors from families like the De Morevils, De Umphravils, De Berkelais, De Quincis, De Viponts and De Vaux.

As the knights settled the boundaries of their vast estates, they took territorial names, as in Hamilton, Moray, Crawford, Cunningham, Dunbar, Ross, Wemyss, Dundas, Galloway, Renfrew, Greenhill, Hazelwood, Sandylands and Church-hill.

Other names, though not with any obvious geographical or topographical features, nevertheless derived from ancient parishes like Douglas, Forbes, Dalyell and Guthrie.

Other surnames were coined in connection with occupations, castles or legendary deeds.

Stuart originated in the word steward, a prestigious post which was an integral part of any large medieval household. The same applied to Cooks, Chamberlains, Constables and Porters.

Borders towns and forts – needed in areas like the Debateable Lands which were constantly fought over by feuding local families – had their own distinctive names; and it was often from them that the resident groups took their communal titles, as in the Grahams of Annandale, the Elliots and Armstrongs of the East Marches, the Scotts and Kerrs of Teviotdale and Eskdale.

Even physical attributes crept into surnames, as in Small, Little and More (the latter being 'beg' in Gaelic), Long or Lang, Stark, Stout, Strong or Strang and even Jolly.

Mieklejohns would have had the strength of several men, while Littlejohn was named after the legendary sidekick of Robin Hood.

Colours got into the act with Black, White, Grey, Brown and Green (Red developed into Reid, Ruddy or Ruddiman). Blue was rare and nobody ever wanted to be associated with yellow.

Pompous worthies took the name Wiseman, Goodman and Goodall.

Words intimating the sons of leading figures were soon affiliated into the language as in Johnson, Adamson, Richardson and Thomson, while the Norman equivalent of Fitz (from the French-Latin 'filius' meaning 'son') cropped up in Fitzmaurice and Fitzgerald.

The prefix 'Mac' was 'son of' in Gaelic and clans often originated with occupations – as in MacNab being sons of the Abbot, MacPherson and MacVicar being sons of the minister and MacIntosh being sons of the chief.

The church's influence could be found in the names Kirk, Clerk, Clarke, Bishop, Friar and Monk. Proctor came from a church official, Singer and Sangster from choristers, Gilchrist and Gillies from Christ's servant, Mitchell, Gilmory and Gilmour from servants of St Michael and Mary, Malcolm from a servant of Columba and Gillespie from a bishop's servant.

The rudimentary medical profession was represented by Barber (a trade which also once included dentistry and surgery) as well as Leech or Leitch.

Businessmen produced Merchants, Mercers, Monypennies, Chapmans, Sellers and Scales, while down at the old village watermill the names that cropped up included Miller, Walker and Fuller.

Other self explanatory trades included – Brewsters and Brewers, Tailors, Saddlers, Wrights, Cartwrights, Smiths, Harpers, Joiners, Sawyers, Masons and Plumbers.

Even the scenery was utilised as in Craig, Moor, Hill, Glen, Wood and Forrest.

Rank, whether high or low, took its place with Laird, Barron, Knight, Tennant, Farmer, Husband, Granger, Grieve, Shepherd, Shearer and Fletcher.

The hunt and the chase supplied Hunter, Falconer, Fowler, Fox, Forrester, Archer and Spearman.

The renowned medieval historian Froissart, who eulogised about the romantic deeds of chivalry (and who condemned Scotland as being a poverty stricken wasteland), once sniffily dismissed the peasantry of his native France as the jacquerie (or the jacques-without-names) but it was these same humble folk who ended up overthrowing the arrogant aristocracy.

In the olden days, only the blueblooded knights of antiquity were entitled to full, proper names, both Christian and surnames, but with the passing of time and a more egalitarian, less feudal atmosphere, more respectful and worthy titles spread throughout the populace as a whole.

Echoes of a far distant past can still be found in most names and they can be borne with pride in commemoration of past generations who fought and toiled in some capacity or other to make our nation what it now is, for good or ill.

Meanwhile, many families proudly boast the heraldic device known as a Coat of Arms, as featured on our front cover.

The central motif of the Coat of Arms would originally have been what was borne on the shield of a warrior to distinguish himself from others on the battlefield.

Not featured on the Coat of Arms, but highlighted on page three, is the family motto and related crest – with the latter frequently different from the central motif.

Chapter two:

Sons of the warriors

The vast majority of law-abiding and peace-loving Wilsons scattered across the globe may be surprised to learn of not only the warlike roots of their surname, but of how a significant number of its bearers figured in some of the most notorious and bloody incidents in Scotland's turbulent history.

The name is a derivative of William, under its popular diminutive of Will. William itself is from the Old German 'Wilhelm' or 'Willihelm', with 'will' denoting the fierce dedication required to overcome one's foes in battle, while 'helm' refers to an armoured 'helmet.'

While the surname Williamson refers to 'son of William', Wilson refers to 'son of Will', and both William and Will became popular names following the Norman Conquest of England in 1066 under the leadership of the mighty William, Duke of Normandy.

In Scotland, however, the name also became popular through its famed monarch William the Lyon, who reigned from 1165 to 1214.

Wilson became a surname through the gradual introduction of hereditary surnames, and variations include Wylson, Wylsone, Willison, Wylie, and Vylsone.

First recorded in Scotland at the dawn of the fifteenth century, it established itself as a common surname particularly in Dumfriesshire, Ayrshire, and the Glasgow and Stirling areas, although concentrations of Wilsons are also found in the Fife and Angus areas.

Records show a Wilson buying the lands of Hinschelwood and Cleugh, at Carnwath, Lanarkshire, in 1653, while his descendant, John Wilson of Airdrie, who lived from 1809 to 1889, was created a baronet in 1906.

In England, the name is particularly commonplace in Devon and Lancashire, while it is a popular name in Northern Ireland, where four out of five Wilsons are believed to be of Scottish descent.

It was through the Plantation of Ulster, from 1603 to 1640, that many Lowland Scots such as Wilsons settled there as part of a government policy to populate the land with British Protestants, at the expense of native Irish Catholics.

The descendants of many of these Wilsons who settled in Ireland later found a new home in North America, where many Wilsons of today may well find they have original Scottish roots, albeit via Ireland.

While Wilsons thrived in the Scottish Lowlands, England, Ireland, and, later, North America, Australia, Canada, and New Zealand, much of the romance and drama associated with the name is to be found in the far-flung Highlands.

Unravelling what is a complex genealogical skein, it is possible to firmly link the Wilsons with the two proud clans of Gunn and Innes.

These links are so strong that Wilsons of today who can trace a descent back to either of these clans are recognised as a sept, or branch, of the clan and can wear its tartan and take pride in its crest and motto.

The tale of how the Wilsons became associated with Clan Gunn is a tragic one, but one that is sadly all too familiar in the bloody history of the clan feuds and treachery that for centuries blighted the Highlands and Islands of Scotland.

'Either peace or war' is the motto of Clan Gunn, while its crest is a hand grasping a sword, rather fitting sentiment and imagery for a clan that claims a descent from Gunni, a grandson of the ferocious Sweyn Asleifson, known to posterity as The Ultimate Viking, who was killed in a raid on Dublin in 1171.

Originally settled near Morvern, in Caithness, in the northeast of Scotland, the Gunns had deadly enemies in Clan Keith and Clan Mackay, both clans defeating the Gunns in battle at Wick in 1438.

Rather ironically, perhaps, 'Williamson' is a recognised sept of Clan Mackay!

Before the mighty Sinclairs were granted the earldom of Caithness in 1455, the Gunns had held the powerful and prestigious position of representing the royal authority throughout this wild and vast area.

This authority in the mid-fifteenth century was represented in the form of the clan chief, George Gunn, known as Crowner ('Coroner') Gunn, the title indicating this royal authority.

In 1464, in a desperate bid to settle a bitter and costly feud with the Keiths, it was arranged that Crowner Gunn and the chief of the Keiths would meet at a chapel near Girnigoe, in Caithness.

Understandably distrustful of one another, it was stipulated that only 'twelve horses' from each side should ride to the meeting.

Arriving first, Crowner Gunn and his eleven clansmen went into the chapel to pray. The Keiths arrived but, treacherously, they had two men to each horse.

Outnumbered by two to one, the Gunns, including Crowner Gunn, were slaughtered in the battle that ensued.

This act of treachery festered in the minds

of the Gunns for so long that seventy years later, in 1534, a grandson of the Crowner exacted revenge by killing George Keith, chief of the Keiths, along with twelve of his men, in a fierce battle at Drummoy.

Earlier, however, following the death of Crowner Gunn and subsequent threats to their existence by the Sinclairs, some of his sons had dispersed from their original homelands.

While some remained in the Braemore area of Caithness, James, William, and Henry Gunn took their kinsfolk and settled in Strathullie, in Sutherland.

Those Gunns who followed William became known as 'the sons of William, or Will', which later developed into the more recognisable anglicised form of 'Wilson.'

Wilsons who can trace a descent to Banffshire, the historic Scottish county now divided between Moray and Aberdeenshire, can claim a link to the Innes family of Littlefield, one of several branches of this clan whose crest is a boar's head and whose motto is 'Be traist', signifying trust.

Berowald, a knight of Flanders renowned for his chivalry and martial prowess, was given the lands of Innes, in Moray, by Malcolm IV, between 1153 and 1165. His grandson later adopted the name of these lands as the family name.

While Wilsons who can trace a descent to Clan Gunn or the Innes's of Littlefield, in Banffshire, have the right to wear their tartan, there is also a specific Wilson tartan.

It was the Wilson family of Bannockburn, near Stirling, merchant weavers from 1750 to 1906, who in 1819 were responsible for compiling the earliest surviving list of tartans.

Known as *The Key Pattern Book of William Wilson and Sons, Bannockburn*, it lists thirty Highland clan tartans, thirteen family tartans, and twelve distinct, or general, tartans.

A Wilson tartan is included among the family tartans and, originally known as 'the Janet Wilson sett', it was created for the wife of the founder of the Wilson company.

Chapter three:

Murder and martyrdom

As the master of robes, or tailor, to the ambitious and ruthless James Hepburn, 4th Earl of Bothwell, Patrick Wilson played a key role in the infamous murder of Henry, Lord Darnley, the spoiled and dissolute husband of the ill-starred Mary, Queen of Scots.

Although the exact circumstances surrounding the assassination are still shrouded in mystery more than 400 years after the event, what is known is that Bothwell was the arch-conspirator, assisted by a number of lesser-known figures, such as the hapless Patrick Wilson, who probably had no choice in the matter.

It was on the evening of February 9, 1567, that a tremendous explosion rudely awoke Edinburgh. Kirk o' Field, a house just within the city walls, had been blown to smithereens, while the bodies of Darnley and his servant were later found in the garden.

Darnley, suffering from what in all probability was syphilis, had been lodged in Kirk o' Field while Mary and her infant son, the future James VI, were in residence at the Palace of Holyrood.

The queen had attended a wedding break-fast at Holyrood for one of her ladies-in-waiting, visiting her husband briefly before returning to the palace for the wedding masque.

In the intervening period the cellar of Kirk o' Field had been packed with gunpowder, furtively transported there by Wilson and others.

When the corpses of Darnley and his servant were discovered, it was noticed both were unmarked by the tremendous blast, and that they had been either strangled or smothered as they attempted to make their escape after belatedly realising their lives were in danger.

Bothwell, who later took the twice-widowed Mary's hand in marriage, was contro-versially acquitted of having had any part in 'the

cruel, odious, treasonable and abominable slaughter' of Darnley, but less powerful figures implicated in the murder, such as Patrick Wilson, were subsequently brought to justice and executed.

A series of incriminating letters between Bothwell and Mary, known as the Casket Letters, suggest the queen may have been implicated in the plot to murder her husband, but controversy still rages as to the authenticity of the letters.

Many horrific acts of cruelty were perpetrated throughout what was known in Scotland as the Killing Time, of 1680 to 1685, and a young Wilson lass from the southwest of Scotland achieved martyrdom in Covenanting circles after suffering a horrific ordeal during this terrible time.

Many hundreds of ordinary people were hunted down, tortured, and killed, for their adherence to the National Covenant, first signed at Greyfriars Church, Edinburgh, in 1638.

Those who subscribed to the Covenant, that pledged to uphold the Presbyterian religion and denied the so-called 'divine right' of kings, were known as Covenanters, and many literally took to the hills to attend open-air religious services known as conventicles.

Margaret Wilson, aged only 18, along with her 13-year-old sister Agnes and 16-year-old brother Thomas, whose father, Gilbert, farmed at Glenvernoch, near Newton Stewart, were classed as rebels because they regularly attended these outlawed conventicles, and sought sanctuary in the bleak hills and moors.

The brother evaded capture, but the sisters were betrayed and captured and, charged with attending conventicles and refusing to accept the authority of the king in matters of religion, were sentenced to death by drowning.

A 63-year-old woman, Margaret Milliken, was sentenced to a similar fate.

Gilbert Wilson desperately petitioned the Privy Council to grant his young daughters a reprieve, but this was only granted to Agnes.

Following widespread public disquiet, however, the Privy Council eventually ordered that Margaret Wilson and Margaret Milliken be released.

Resenting this interference in their affairs the local authority in Wigtown insisted the executions go ahead and, on May 11, 1685, the two women were taken onto the Solway Sands at low tide and tied to stakes.

Both were given the opportunity to gain a last minute reprieve if they agreed to pray for the king, but they obdurately refused. Their heads were viciously pushed under the rapidly rising tidal waters with the soldiers' halberds, and held there until they drowned.

More than 50 years later, in 1736, another Wilson, although of totally different character from the pious Margaret Wilson, became the focal point of another notorious incident which this time led to the infamous civil disturbance in Edinburgh known as the Porteous Riot.

Smugglers were very much the Robin Hoods of their day in eighteenth century Scotland, admired for their audacious flouting of the excise laws and consequent popularity as purveyors of goods at a cheap price.

One such smuggler was Andrew Wilson,

a former baker and seaman who, after settling in Fife, turned to the much more lucrative but dangerous career of outwitting the excisemen.

Wilson had for some time suffered from persistent harassment from a particularly officious commissioner of customs in Kirkcaldy and, along with two other men, exacted vengeance in the spring of 1736 by waylaying him, beating him up, and robbing him.

One of the men later informed on Wilson and his other accomplice, George Robertson, and the pair were tried and sentenced to be hanged.

As was customary with condemned men, they were taken under heavy guard for a final church service, in Edinburgh's St. Giles' Kirk.

Wilson, described as large and powerful, managed to grab two of his guards and, before shouting to Robertson to make a run for it from the kirk, seized another by the collar with his teeth.

The sympathetic congregation helped Robertson to flee, and he was never seen again. Wilson was not so fortunate, however, when he was taken from the town's Tolbooth three days later and publicly hanged.

A furious crowd had attempted to cut the popular smuggler down from the scaffold as his body jerked in its final death throes, and Captain John Porteous, the unpopular captain of the city guard, fired on them with his musket.

The city guard followed his lead, and after only a few short minutes nine people lay dead and twenty wounded, some of them who had been innocent onlookers.

Porteous was found to have grossly exceeded his authority and was sentenced to be hanged for murder, but on the day of his execution, September 7, 1736, word spread that he had been granted a reprieve, pending a full pardon.

This news inflamed the mob, who dragged him from his captivity in the Tolbooth and unceremoniously hanged him from the pole of a nearby shop. No one was ever punished for this exercise in mob justice, but the town itself was fined £2,000.

Chapter four:

Politics and pop

A more widespread civil disturbance, one that had fatal consequences for a James Wilson, a weaver from Strathaven, in Lanarkshire, occurred in 1820.

Wilson, along with John Baird and Andrew Hardie was hanged and beheaded for his part in the Radical Rising of that year, which had followed the posting of a proclamation in Glasgow calling for a general strike in support of much needed political reform.

Wilson had been inspired by the English writer and activist Thomas Paine, who had not only advocated, in his *The Rights of Man*, equality and justice for all, but had campaigned for colonial America's independence from Britain.

Also influenced by the ideas of Paine was another James Wilson, a farmer's son from Carskedy, Fife, who immigrated to America in 1766, aged 22.

After studying and practicing law he became a member of congress for Pennsylvania, and was one of the signatories of the American Declaration of Independence of 1776 and one of the framers of the American Constitution of 1787.

A contemporary of James Wilson had been Samuel Wilson, who holds the distinction of being responsible for America's rather unusual surname of 'Uncle Sam.'

Born in 1766, he ran a meat packing plant in New York until his death in 1854. His main customer was the United States Army and all meat packed and shipped to the troops was stamped 'U.S.'

Troops joked the 'U.S.', rather than indicating 'United States', actually stood for 'Uncle Sam' Wilson, and the nickname stuck!

Two Wilsons who made significant impacts on the politics of their respective nations were Woodrow Wilson and Harold Wilson.

Born in Staunton, Virginia, of Scottish and Irish descent in 1856, Thomas Woodrow

Wilson served two consecutive terms, from 1913 to 1921, as American President.

In 1920, four years before his death, he was awarded the Nobel Peace Prize for his role in establishing the League of Nations in the aftermath of the First World War.

Harold Wilson, born in 1916, and who died in 1995, was the British Labour Party politician who served as Prime Minister during three separate terms throughout the 1960s and 1970s.

Created Lord Wilson of Rievaulx after his retirement from politics, he was also a founder of the Open University.

Born in Paisley, in Scotland, in 1766, Alexander Wilson became known as the father of American ornithology after emigrating from Scotland in 1794, while in the world of science Charles T.R. Wilson (1869-1959) was the British scientist who won the Nobel Prize for Physics in 1927 for his construction of a cloud chamber for photographing particles from outer space.

In more contemporary times, Wilson is

the surname of brothers Brian, Denis, and Carl, born and raised in Los Angeles, and who achieved international fame, along with their cousin Mike Love and friend Al Jardine, as The Beach Boys, releasing their first album in 1961.

A string of hits followed, and they were inducted into the prestigious Rock n' Roll Hall of fame in 1988.